"Hello Toes!

Movement Games for Children

by Anne Lief Barlin [and] Nurit Kalev."

Princeton Book Co. c 1989

Copyright © 1989 by Anne Lief Barlin and Nurit Kalev

A Dance Horizons Book
Princeton Book Company, Publishers
POB 57
Pennington, NJ 08534

Cover Design by Main Street Design
Interior Design by Roxanne Barrett

Library of Congress Cataloging-in-Publication Data

Barlin, Anne Lief.
    Hello toes : movement games for children / by Anne Lief Barlin and
Nurit Kalev.
        p.   cm.
    "A Dance Horizons book."
    ISBN 0-916622-88-6
     1. Movement education. 2. Dancing—Children's dances. 3. Games.
4. Children and adults. I. Kalev, Nurit. II. Title.
GV452.B365   1989
793'.01922—dc20   89-35995
                                                                        CIP

By the Same Author

Contents

Foreword

In 1961 I signed up for my first dance class. I had never taken dance before because I was afraid I might not be good at it, or, worse yet, I might have a teacher who was harsh and critical. None of my fears were realized in Anne Barlin's class. I felt completely comfortable; we all moved in our own way, at our own pace. Anne provided activities we needed to stretch and strengthen our bodies; direction and motivation for moving creatively; and support and encouragement for everything we did. Dance was a lot of fun!

Over the years since then I have been Anne Barlin's student, colleague, and friend. I have watched her work with many groups in the same positive ways that she worked with me in that first class. I have observed and participated in teacher workshops in which she taught the positive attitudes and skills needed to provide effective creative movement activities for children (Anne has worked with teachers all over the United States and in Japan and Israel). Best of all I have watched Anne inspire and delight children as they develop new skills, coordination, and confidence in using their bodies.

When I tried to analyze what Anne does that makes her work so successful, I realized that she always begins by creating what I call a "psychologically safe space": an environment full of love, humor, and support. She lets her students know that she accepts them, that their ways of moving are just fine with her, and that she would never judge or compare negatively. Once trust has been established she can provide activities that are challenging and that develop strength, skill, and creativity. Creativity does not develop in a vacuum (it rarely works to put on music and say, "Now be creative."), and one of Anne's special gifts is knowing how to create the kinds of structures that help creativity flourish.

Today we have become aware of the importance of the very early years in children's development. The body is the child's connection to the world. Physical well-being is essential to all other aspects of development. A sensitive, strong, flexible coordinated body allows a child to function competently in the world. Like all other areas of development, physical development can be enhanced by the right kind of early experiences.

In this new book, Anne Barlin (with co-author Nurit Kalev) turns her attention to the kinds of activities that parents can do with very young children to enhance their physical development. In it, she shares her unique approach to moving with children. She begins, as she always does, by helping the parent to create a safe and loving environment in which children can develop awarness of their bodies, physical skills, and creativity. The activities are simple and can be done in a spirit of enjoyment, can help to strengthen bonds between parent and child, shape positive attitudes toward movement, and help to assure the optimal physical development of young children. Every parent can benefit from Anne Barlin's years of experience in bringing joyful movement experiences to children; and every child can benefit from early, positive movement experiences.

Stephanie Feeney
Professor of Education
University of Hawaii

Preface

As my students grew with me through early childhood into their adolescence and then their adulthood, I began to wonder. "Is it a coincidence? Do only extremely intelligent children stay on to study with me? Or is it the other way around? Can this kind of training develop not only superior movement skills but also an unusual intellegence?" I began to observe very carefully.

Now, more than 50 years later, I know. I know that superior intelligence was developing simultaneously with superior body skills. And I know that the reason the process was working was because — along with brain and body development — self-esteem was growing, a confidence that catapulted that young person high above the average.

Parents, you have a great opportunity. Through your child's eyes you are the model of perfection. Your every word of encouragement, every smile of approval, carries great weight. Give that encouragement and approval freely. Help your child to take those first steps toward success.

Children need to succeed. Success is an essential ingredient in their growth and development. As you express your enthusiasm and excitement, and as your children feel their bodies getting stronger, and finding a new balance, their joy and excitement leads them forward. The small successes lead to larger ones. Their confidence grows, and as it grows, they try even harder. And the harder they work, the more skillful they become. Be patient. It is a gradual and exciting process: an interplay between mind, body, and spirit. You are an essential part of that process. The successes belong to both of you.

How to Use This Book

Hello Toes is a book of movement and dance games for adults and children to perform *together*. Through these activities, both parent and child will discover new things about themselves and their world.

The book is divided into three sections. In the first part, games using common household objects—brooms, blocks, balloons, cloth, elastic, and so on—are described. The idea is that you don't need fancy toys or special equipment to have fun with your child. In Part Two, the objects are put away and the imagination comes into play. Here the child and adult have a chance to experience the body through different movements, such as sliding, swinging, twirling, and somersaults.

Finally, there is a selection of dance stories and rhythmic chants that are longer and more complex than the games in the first two parts of this book. The parent and child have a chance to create a total dance work, and to experience dance songs from different cultures, including Africa, Japan, and the southern U.S. The book ends with a "quiet time" activity, a time of rest and contemplation for both adult and child.

This is not a book for the parent or child to read from cover to cover. You should explore the text, experimenting with the different activities, developing your own variations and interpretations of these dance games. Don't sit in a chair and read it; take a minute to scan a page and then get up on your feet with your child and enjoy!

About Musical Accompaniment

We have prepared a special cassette tape including some of our favorite folk dance and classical pieces to accompany some of the dance and movement games in this book. You may find that using this tape will give you some good ideas from which you can experiment further with records from your own collection or from your local library. We've indicated in the text when music is available for an exercise on the cassette. For some of the exercises, no musical accompaniment is given; however, it is always more fun to move to music. You can experiment with using different selections on the tape to accompany the different games, or if you own my book *Teaching Your Wings to Fly*, you will find that much of the music is suitable for the exercises. You can also try other musical styles that you and your child enjoy.

There are several different games in the book that are called "Freeze & Move." On the cassette tape, we have taken short snippets of diffrent kinds of music—fast, slow, happy, sad, loud, soft— and left gaps where the child will "freeze" during the game. If you don't have the cassette, you could make your own tape from your own record collection, leaving gaps for the "freeze" parts. Or, you could play a musical instrument, hum, clap a rhythm, or sing a melody, stopping appropriately and saying "freeze." We're sure you'll develop many innovative ways to play "Freeze & Move."

For the dance games at the end of the book, there are specific songs that accompany these movements. These songs are given on the cassette tape, but you may also find them in children's song-books or records in your library.

Anne L. Barlin

PART ONE:
Games Using Objects

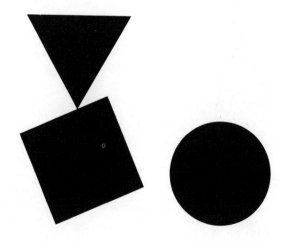

Balloons

<table>
<tr><td colspan="3">WHAT YOUR CHILD WILL GAIN FROM THIS EXPERIENCE</td></tr>
<tr><td>PHYSICAL</td><td>COGNITIVE</td><td>EMOTIONAL/SOCIAL</td></tr>
<tr><td>Full body stretch
Stomach muscle
  strength
Use of alternate hands
  & feet
Spatial awareness
Tactile sense
Balance
Locating body parts
Coordination</td><td>Responding to verbal
  instructions
Naming body parts
Learning concepts of
  "over," "under," &
  "through"
Aesthetic awareness</td><td>Learning to be gentle
Adult/child relationship
Sense of humor
Enthusiasm
Joy</td></tr>
</table>

● You Need

A large, round, blown-up balloon for each of you. Be prepared with some spares in case of popping.

● Balloon Toss

ADULT &
CHILD

Throw the balloon to each other.

Gently kick the balloon to each other.

Sit back to back and send it over your head from behind.

Send it to each other between your legs.

How else can you toss the balloon to each other?

Accompaniment: "Invisible Strings" (A, 1)

● Naming Body Parts

ADULT

Sit on the floor with the child and say: *"When I say, 'head,' touch your balloon to my head."*

"When I say, 'elbow,' touch your balloon to my elbow." Mention as many parts as possible including shoulder, finger, wrist, back, neck, ear, etc.

CHILD — Now it's your turn. Name a body part and the adult's balloon will touch it.

● Reach the Balloon

ADULT — Hold your balloon just high enough to require the child to stretch upward fully.

CHILD — Touch the balloon with your hand; now with the other hand.

Jump and touch the balloon: first with one hand, then with the other, then with both hands.

ADULT — The child under two years of age will have difficulty jumping. Encourage, but don't insist. Ability will come gradually as you repeat the various exercises

● Over the Moon-Balloon

ADULT — Lay the balloon on the floor. Demonstrate how to step over the balloon.

CHILD — Hold the adult's hand, then step carefully over the balloon.

Now step over with the other foot.

Hold both of the adult's hands and jump over the balloon.

● Football-oon

ADULT & CHILD — Sit on the floor together, and begin with either the adult or child going first.

4

Hold the balloon between your feet and pass it to the other. The other accept it with *the feet only*. Reverse.

Pass the balloon with your feet, the other accept it with the hands. Reverse.

Pass the balloon with your hands, the other accept it with the feet. Reverse.

● Under the Bridge

ADULT   Create a bridge with your body by standing with your legs far enough apart to allow the balloon to roll through.

Or place one hand and one foot on the ground.

Or place two hands and one foot on the ground.

Enjoy exploring more possibilities.

CHILD   Roll your balloon under the bridge.

Roll your balloon and then crawl after it under the bridge.

Blow your balloon under the bridge

● Balloon Balance

ADULT &
CHILD

Holding the same balloon with only one of your hands, walk together forward and backward.

Change hands and walk. Now dance, keeping the balloon balanced between you.

Can you also balance the balloon between your heads? Between other parts of your body?

Accompaniment: "Invisible Strings" (A, 1)

● Volleyball-oon

ADULT &
CHILD

Bounce your balloon into the air without letting it fall to the ground.

Share one balloon and take turns tapping it to keep it in the air.

Can you keep it in the air by tapping it with different parts of your body?

● Balloon Jump

ADULT &
CHILD
Place your own balloon between your knees and jump. Hold it gently. Feel its softness

Blocks

WHAT YOUR CHILD WILL GAIN FROM THIS EXPERIENCE		
PHYSICAL Balance Exercising the tactile sense Eye-foot coordination Foot awareness	COGNITIVE Directional awareness Spatial awareness	EMOTIONAL/SOCIAL Confidence Joy Pride Self-reliance

▲ You Need

At least two wooden blocks. They need to be small enough for the child to pick up, yet large and strong enough for the child to stand on them.

▲ Block Jump

CHILD

Place two blocks side by side. Jump or leap over them.

Separate the blocks a little bit. Jump or leap over both blocks at the same time. Keep widening the space to see how big a jump you can make.

Place one block on top of the other and jump or leap over it.

If you have more than two blocks, make a tower to see how high you can jump.

ADULT

For many of these activities, the child may need your help. Start by holding both of the child's hands. When you feel the confidence growing, hold one hand and then the other.

▲ Block Skate

ADULT   You need a smooth floor for this activity. A rug or carpet will not work.

Hold both of the child's hands. Face the child and walk backward, matching your steps to the child's steps.

CHILD   Hold both of the adult's hands. Stand on top of the two blocks and slide them forward as if you are skating.

▲ Freeze & Move

CHILD   Scatter your blocks on the floor around the room.

When the music plays, dance or move around the blocks. When the music stops, step onto a block and make a statue.

Accompaniment: "Freeze & Move" (A, 2)

▲ Blind Walk

ADULT   Hold the child's hand for both parts of the Blind Walk. Then let the child hold your hand while you do the activity.

CHILD   Close your eyes and move around the blocks without touching them.

Close your eyes and walk on top of the blocks.

▲ Balances

CHILD   As you walk, try to balance the block on different parts of your body: your head, hand (palm & back), shoulder, back, foot, etc.

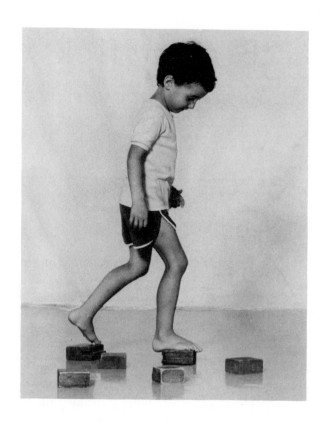

▲ Stepping Stones

CHILD   Place as many blocks as you have in a straight line with enough space between each one for your foot.

Step onto each block, giving each foot a turn.

Step over each block, onto the floor, giving each foot a turn.

Try stepping onto and over the blocks backwards, then sideways on each side.

Walk, snaking between the blocks.

Make a full circle around each block before moving on to the next one.

Broomstick

■ You Need

A broomstick and a rug or mat for safety.

■ Broomstick Climb

ADULT — Stand on the rug or mat, and with two hands, hold the stick parallel to the floor. Hold it low enough for the child to grasp.

Place your hands on top of the child's hands and lift the stick slightly off the ground.

Repeat this a few times until you see the child's confidence growing.

Do the broomstick exercise for only a few minutes. It can become too much of a strain on the child's arms and shoulders. Watch for the first sign of fatigue and go on to something else.

CHILD — While you are up in the air and hanging onto the stick, try lifting one leg to touch your toe to the stick.

Give each leg a turn.

Chairs

WHAT YOUR CHILD WILL GAIN FROM THIS EXPERIENCE		
PHYSICAL Balance Spatial awareness Motor skills Full body strength Full body stretch	COGNITIVE Naming body parts Naming colors Improvisation Responding to music Spatial awareness	EMOTIONAL/SOCIAL Confidence Caring Relating to others Being sensitive to others

● You Need

One chair for both of you to share. Be sure that it is steady and solid; that it has a flat seat, and, if possible, space underneath it.

● Chair Jump

CHILD Stand on the chair. The adult will hold you as you jump off.

Now try different ways of jumping off: start on one foot and jump; then the other foot; hold your hands on the chair and jump off backwards; jump off on the other side of the chair, etc.

ADULT Help the child in whatever way you are needed.

● Gift Wrapping

ADULT Say to the child: *"Pretend that the chair is a present for your good friend and that your body is beautiful gift-wrapping paper."*

"Wrap the whole chair with your whole body. What color is your paper?"

"Now I am the beautiful ribbon. What color should I be?"

"I'm wrapping myself around the paper and making a beautiful bow."

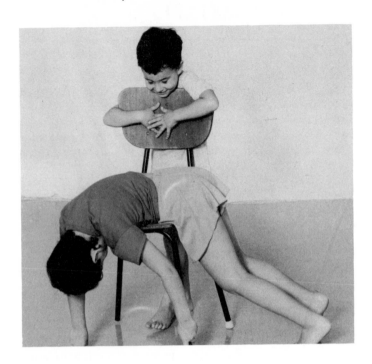

● Chair Dance

ADULT   Select some music that the child enjoys dancing to, or you can sing or hum.

Stand close and be ready to help if the child loses balance.

CHILD   Stand on top of the chair and dance.

● Direction Game

ADULT   Stand on opposite sides of the chair and say: *"I am putting my hand on the seat; now under the seat; now on the back of the chair; on the legs,"* etc.

"Now its your turn. I'll mention a part of the chair and you touch it."

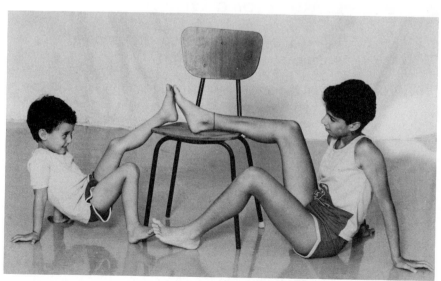

| ADULT & CHILD | This time you are on the floor with the chair between you. Name the body parts and try to touch each other's elbows, heads, noses, then toes *under* the chair, to the *back* of the chair, etc. What other parts can you touch? |

● Freeze & Move

ADULT	Make sure to hold the child firmly while he or she is dancing on the chair.
ADULT & CHILD	Dance around the chair while the music is playing; when the music stops, freeze into a statue that is touching the chair.
CHILD	Now, stand on the chair; When the music plays, dance on the chair. When it stops, make a statue that is standing on the chair.
ADULT & CHILD	Now the chair is the statue, but it was never finished. So when you freeze this time, both of you become part of the statue and make it complete.

Accompaniment: "Freeze & Move" (A, 2)

● Freeze & Move for a Group

ADULTS & CHILDREN	Use as many chairs as there are children, and scatter them around the room.
CHILDREN	When the music is playing, dance in and out and around the chairs. Each time the music stops, land on top of a different chair, making a new statue.
ADULTS	Remove half of the original number of chairs. When the music is playing, the children dance; when it stops, one child sits on a chair and freezes while another child freezes under the chair. Positions and partners change with each repetition.
	To avoid accidents, ask the children to sit slowly and carefully onto the chair and *never* to stand.

Cloth

WHAT YOUR CHILD WILL GAIN FROM THIS EXPERIENCE		
PHYSICAL Muscle activation in the feet, legs, hands, shoulders, and back. Tactile sense Balance	COGNITIVE Concentration Organization Motor planning Naming body parts	SOCIAL/EMOTIONAL Cooperation Confidence Fun!

▲ You Need

A large piece of material. An old sheet or light table cloth will be fine.

▲ Footsies

ADULT & CHILD

Spread the cloth on the floor, and try to walk on it without making wrinkles.

Now make wrinkles.

With your toes only, each grasp one end of the cloth. Pull backwards, away from each other, stretching the cloth.

▲ Trampoline

ADULT & CHILD

Stand and hold two corners of the cloth.

Put a ball, balloon, or a stuffed animal in the center of the cloth, and roll it back and forth to each other.

Toss the ball or object into the air and catch it on the cloth.

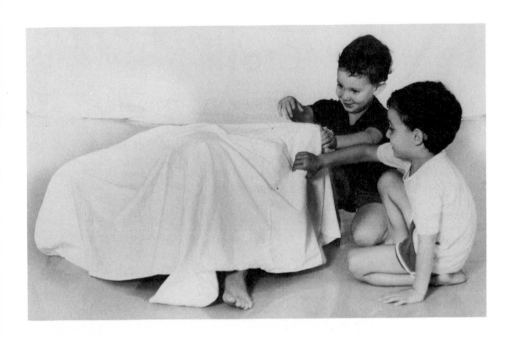

▲ Hide and Seek

ADULT   Close your eyes.

CHILD   Hide under the cloth.

ADULT   Open your eyes, and through the cloth, touch one part of the child's body and name it; then touch and name another part, and another.

Now change roles.

▲ Wagon

CHILD   Lie down in the center of the cloth.

ADULT   Pull the child slowly around the room.

▲ Turtle

ADULT &   Go under the cloth together. You are on your
CHILD   hands and kees. You are a turtle, and the cloth is your shell. Crawl together, keeping your shell on your backs. Don't let it slip.

▲ Cocoon

ADULT   Lie at one end of the cloth. Hold one corner of the cloth as you roll yourself to the other end, creating a cocoon.

Crawl out of the cocoon trying not to change its shape.

Now roll the child in the cloth.

Ask the child to crawl out as you did, without changing the shape of the cocoon.

▲ Finale

ADULT &   Together, fold the cloth.
CHILD

Crepe Paper

WHAT YOUR CHILD WILL GAIN FROM THIS EXPERIENCE		
PHYSICAL Balance Coordination Tactile sense Learning to be gentle & careful	COGNITIVE Measuring Problem solving Academic learning ability	SOCIAL/EMOTIONAL Self-Esteem Trust Confidence

▲ You Need

A streamer of crepe paper about five feet long for each of you. Choose your favorite color.

▲ Trust Walk

ADULT & CHILD Place your streamers on the floor anywhere in the room.

CHILD Close your eyes.

ADULT Stand behind the child and place your hand on his or her shoulder. Carefully lead the child through the streamers being careful not to touch them.

CHILD Now you lead the adult.

▲ Change the Size

ADULT & CHILD Unroll your streamer and lay it flat on the ground. You may wish to put a book on one end to hold it down.

Walk on the streamer. Use your arms to help you balance.

Using only your feet, make it very short.

Using only one hand, make it long again.

Using only your head, make it short again.

▲ Jump-overs

*ADULT &
CHILD*

Jump over the streamer without touching it.

Find different ways of jumping: two feet; one foot; cross-over; or land with the streamer between your feet.

The older child can jump and turn in the air.

▲ Balancing

*ADULT &
CHILD*

Put your streamer on your head letting the ends hang down. Try to walk and balance the streamer without touching it with your hands.

▲ Blowing

ADULT &
CHILD

Go to different ends of the room with your streamers. Find a comfortable position on the floor and blow them across the floor to each other.

▲ Moving Streamers

ADULT &
CHILD

Hold one end of the streamer and walk. Let the rest of the streamer drag on the floor. Be careful not to step on the other's streamer.

Walk, holding one end of your streamer high in the air. Let the rest fly behind you.

Run with the streamer flying behind you.

▲ Sharing

ADULT & Use only one streamer.
CHILD
While each of you holds one end of the streamer, slowly walk together being careful not to tear the streamer.

Play music or sing, and dance with each other without tearing the streamer.

Drum

WHAT YOUR CHILD WILL GAIN FROM THIS EXPERIENCE		

PHYSICAL
Full body stretch
Spatial awareness
Eye-hand coordination
Leg strength
Tactile sense
Stamina
	COGNITIVE
	Specialization of each
	   side of the body &
	   brain
	Motor planning
	Measuring
		EMOTIONAL/SOCIAL
		Confidence
		Fun!

● You Need

A drum, tambourine, or bell, or anything that will make a lovely sound when the child jumps and hits it; and a good floor with spring. If your floor is not made of wood, then a heavy rug or mat will do.

● Drum Jump

ADULT   Stand in the middle of the room. Hold the drum just high enough so that the child must jump and stretch to reach and hit the drum. Do not go beyond the point where the child can reach.

CHILD   Jump and hit the drum with one hand. Now try to hit it with the other hand. Jump a few times giving each hand a turn. (Give a little extra practice to the hand that did not hit as hard.)

This time, start at the end of the room. Run until you get to the drum, then jump and hit it. Now try it from the other side of the room with the other hand.

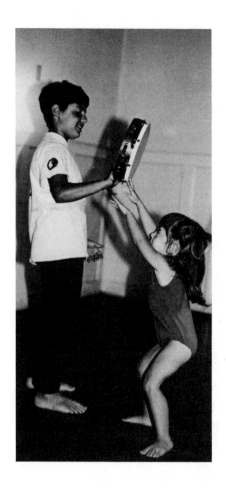

Now start at the end of the room again and run to the drum, but this time, *before* you jump, turn yourself around and hit the drum!

ADULT   If the child does not voluntarily use the other hand, don't make an issue out of it. Eventually, as the child matures, he or she will do it with ease. Encouragement is all that is needed.

Success and the joy it brings will motivate the child to do this exercise again and again. Consistent practice will create the strength, stamina, and confidence that will lead the child to take on greater challenges.

Elastic

WHAT YOUR CHILD WILL GAIN FROM THIS EXPERIENCE		
PHYSICAL *Full body stretch* *Spatial awareness* *Awareness of body parts*	*COGNITIVE* *Problem solving* *Decision making*	*SOCIAL/EMOTIONAL* *Cooperation* *Interdependence* *Fun!*

■ You Need

One piece of soft elastic, about six to eight feet long, stretched and tied to two heavy solid objects like a table, a heavy chair, or a piano.

■ Reaching

*ADULT &
CHILD*

Lift the elastic as high as you can. Because the adult is naturally taller, the child will be motivated to reach onto tip toe and fully extend the whole body.

■ Bridges

ADULT

Hold the middle of the elastic and stretch it to the height of your waist to create an elastic "bridge" for the child.

CHILD

Try different ways of going under the bridge: crawl; walk; run; go backward; or jump. Think of other ways of going under the bridge.

ADULT

Hold the elastic *down* so that the child can experiment with ways of going *over* it.

Now slowly lift and lower the elastic. As you change the level of the elastic, the child is being challenged to make decisions about going over or under and in what manner.

■ Body Parts

ADULT &
CHILD

Lower the elastic to the floor and stand on it.

Now try holding the elastic down to the floor with other parts of your body: your knees; head; back; stomach; shoulder; or elbow.

Use your whole body to hold down the elastic.

■ Snap

ADULT &
CHILD

Hold the elastic and walk backward, stretching the elastic as far as it will go.

On the count of three, let go!

■ Elastic Dance

ADULT &
CHILD

Play some music, or sing a tune you can dance to together.

As you dance, hold on to either end of the elastic.

Stretch the elastic by dancing far away from each other; loosen it by dancing close together.

Turn, winding the elastic around yourself.

■ Spider's Webs

ADULT Stretch the elastic around various pieces of furniture, making it look like a spider's web.

CHILD The room is full of spider's webs. Without touching them, try to go under and over them.

Now, you are the spider. Catch the elastic with different parts of your body. Stretch it in different directions. Pretend that you are spinning your web.

ADULT Continue to create different forms with the elastic. Encourage the child to play through the forms.

Furniture

WHAT YOUR CHILD WILL GAIN FROM THIS EXPERIENCE		
PHYSICAL Coordination Isolating, locating & naming body parts Spatial awareness Kinesthetic awareness	COGNITIVE Problem solving Motor planning Responding to music Listening skills	EMOTIONAL/SOCIAL Self-discipline Multicultural experience Fun!

▲ You Need

The furniture that is already in the room; it need not be moved.

▲ Freeze & Move

ADULT

While the music is playing, call out the name of one part of the child's body: hand; head; elbow; knee; etc.

CHILD

While the music is playing, walk or dance around the room without touching any of the furniture. When the music stops, touch the nearest piece of furniture with the body part that was called and freeze like a statue.

ADULT

Each time the music plays call a different part. Encourage the child to hold absolutely still as a statue.

Feeling the contrast between movement and total stillness helps to develop a strong kinesthetic sense and self-discipline.

Accompaniment: "Freeze & Move" (A, 2)

Hoops

WHAT YOUR CHILD WILL GAIN FROM THIS EXPERIENCE		
PHYSICAL	COGNITIVE	SOCIAL/EMOTIONAL
Spatial awareness	Aesthetic awareness	Interdependence
Coordination &	Counting	Fun!
isolating body parts	Measuring	
Foot coordination	Learning ability	
	Problem solving	
	Responding to music	

● You Need

A hoop for each of you. The colorful, plastic hula hoop is best.

● 1−2−3 !

ADULT &
CHILD

Hold your hoops flat using two hands high overhead. Your arms are open wide and your elbows are straight. Look up into the center of the hoop.

Slowly count "1−2−3!" and, on the count of "3," open your fingers (your arms remain reaching upward) and let the hoop drop to the floor.

You are now standing in the middle of the hoop. Slowly bend down and lower your arms to touch the hoop.

Slowly lift the hoop and rise until you are standing once again with the hoop high overhead. Repeat several times.

Accompaniment: "Invisible Strings" (A, 1)

● Signal Game

ADULT   Hold the hoop high over your head.

CHILD   Watch the adult carefully. When the hoop is overhead, that is your signal to dance or move around the room.

ADULT   Lower the hoop and stand it on its edge on the floor.

CHILD   When the hoop is lowered, that is your signal to crawl through the hoop.

Keep watching the hoop.

ADULT   Let the child crawl through the hoop a few times before lifting it again.

● Freeze & Move

ADULT &
CHILD　　　Place one hoop only flat on the ground and stand together in the center of the hoop.

When the music plays, step out of the hoop and dance or move around the room by yourself. When the music stops, jump into the center of the hoop together and freeze. Repeat a few times.

ADULT　　　This time, when the music stops, call out a specific body part: leg; hand; head; elbow; etc.

CHILD　　　When the music stops, touch the part of your body that was called *inside* of the hoop and freeze. When the music starts again, move again.

Accompaniment: "Freeze & Move" (A, 2)

● Freeze & Move for a Group

ADULT　　　Place the hoops flat on the floor. They should be spread around the room so that there is enough space to move around them.

CHILDREN　　When the music is playing, dance around the room outside of the hoops. When the music stops, jump into a hoop and freeze.

ADULT　　　Allow the game to continue while you count the number of hoops and the number of children.

Remove as many hoops as needed to end up with twice as many children as hoops.

Say to the children: *"This time, when the music stops, there will be two children in each hoop."*

Then remove more hoops, and say, *"This time, there will be three children,"* then *four*, etc. See how many children can fit into one hoop!

Let the children do their own counting.

Accompaniment: "Freeze & Move" (A, 2)

● Inside/Outside for a Group

ADULTS   Place the hoops flat on the floor. Use as many hoops as you have room for, allowing enough space between them for the children to move around them freely.

CHILDREN   Dance around the room, moving only outside of the hoops.

ADULTS   This time, place the hoops as close as possible, so that they are touching.

CHILDREN   This time, move and dance only inside the hoops.

● Dance with the Hoop

ADULT &   Stand in the middle of your hoop and lift it slowly
CHILD   overhead.

Hold the hoop with either one or two hands, and as you move it, move with it in as many ways as you can: step in and out of it; lower it from overhead or lift it from the ground; lie on the floor and move your legs inside it; etc.

Move smoothly, making each movement a part of your dance.

Accompaniment: "Invisible Strings" (A, 1)

● Hoop Sculptures

ADULT   Arrange two hoops to create a kind of sculpture that forms passages for the child to wander through.

After the child has moved through one, create another.

CHILD   Now it's your turn to make a hoop sculpture for the adult to wander through.

● Circus Hoop

ADULT   Hold your hoop upright, so that the child can pass through it like a circus animal.

CHILD   Find different ways of going through the hoop. You can run, walk, skip, crawl, move in slow motion, go backwards, or head first.

ADULT   Now try holding two hoops upright and parallel. Allow enough space between them for the child to choose to go through both or in and out and around each one.

                Encourage the child to explore different movements.

● Twirling

ADULT &   Stand at opposite ends of the room. The child has
CHILD   a hoop, the adult does not.

CHILD   Get inside the hoop, and holding it with two
            hands, lift it to your waist.

            Look into the adult's eyes and twirl, moving
            gradually towards the adult.

ADULT   Kneel on one knee, and open your arms wide.
            Smile and call the child to come to you.

            When the child arrives, duck under and into the
            hoop. Let the hoop fall around both of you and
            give each other a hug.

            Accompaniment: "Twirling" (A, 3)

Moving Toy

WHAT YOUR CHILD WILL GAIN FROM THIS EXPERIENCE		
PHYSICAL Body suppleness Coordination	COGNITIVE Problem solving Motor planning Stretching the imagination	EMOTIONAL/SOCIAL Sensitivity to others Joy Exhilaration

▲ You Need

A toy that rolls when it is pulled by a string: an animal on wheels; a car; etc.

▲ Moving Toy

ADULT

Hold the string and demonstrate how the toy follows you as you walk, then allow the child to walk and move the toy. The child will feel the string connecting his or her movements with the movement of the toy.

Say to the child: *"Pretend that you are a toy, and I am tying a pretend string to you. Now, I am pulling you. You can move any way that you like: you can walk or crawl; you can sit moving your feet in front of you . . . How else can you move? Watch me, so you know which way the string is pulling you."*

Watch the child's movements carefully so that you go as slowly as the child can move comfortably.

CHILD

Now it's your turn. Let the adult pretend to be the toy and you pull it.

36

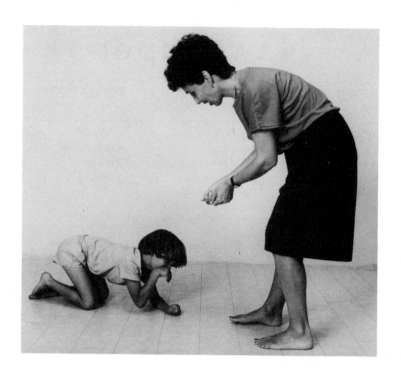

▲ Flying Kite

ADULT   Say to the child: *"You are a kite, and I am tying a string to you. I must hold my end of the string tightly because the kite is flying high up into the air"; "I must watch you very carefully because you might get caught in a tree"; "Watch me to see if I am pulling you in or letting you out"; "What shape is this kite?"*

The action continues as you make various suggestions for interesting interplay between yourself and the child.

Reverse roles.

Newspaper

WHAT YOUR CHILD WILL GAIN FROM THIS EXPERIENCE		
PHYSICAL	COGNITIVE	EMOTIONAL/SOCIAL
Tactile sense	Measuring	Cooperation
Auditory sense	Verbal articulation	Patience
Spatial awareness	Listening skills	Fun!
Foot articulation	Music terminology	
Flexibility	Aesthetic awareness	

■ You Need

A double large sheet of newspaper for both the child and the adult, and bare feet.

■ Paper Sounds

ADULT   Think of three different sounds that you can make with the paper. Ask the child to close his or her eyes then repeat each sound at least three times.

CHILD   Close your eyes and listen to the first sound. Can you imagine how it was made? Open your eyes and tell the adult how the sound was made. Try to make the sound with your newspaper.

Now listen to the other sounds.

■ Paper No-Touch

ADULT &   Find different ways of moving around the paper
CHILD   without touching it. For instance, make a bridge over it or jump over it in as many ways as you can.

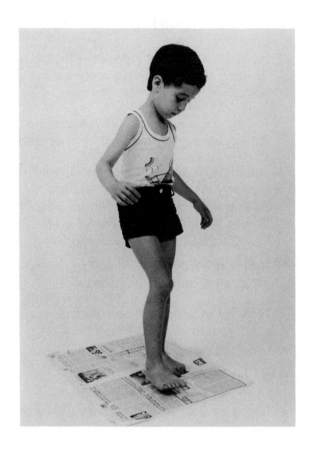

■ Paper Walk

ADULT &
CHILD

Spread your newspaper flat on the floor and stand on it.

Walk on the paper without making a sound. Feel the texture and the temperature with your feet.

Now try to make a sound with your feet. Make as many different sounds as you can.

■ Paper Wind

ADULT &
CHILD

With two hands, hold the corners of the paper and walk. Flap the paper like a gentle wind.

■ Paper/Sound Movements

ADULT   Hold the ends of the paper with two hands. Make a short, sharp, jerky movement tearing the paper about an inch at a time.

CHILD   As you hear each tear, make a sharp, jerky movement with some part of your body.

ADULT   This time, tear the paper slowly and smoothly, and ask the child to move smoothly with the tear. Alternate between short, sharp sounds and longer, smooth sounds creating your own rhythm. The child will respond appropriately.

                Make new sounds by flapping, swinging, crunching, and jiggling the paper.

CHILD   Now it's your turn to tear the paper while the adult makes the movements.

■ Freeze & Move

ADULT &   Using only your feet, tear the newspaper into little
CHILD   pieces and, on your hands and knees, blow the pieces around the room. Now you are ready to begin the game.

                When the music plays, dance around the room; when it stops, pick up a piece of paper with each foot (toes only), then bring the paper up to your hands and make a little ball of it. Each time the music plays, dance again; when it stops, pick up more paper with your toes and add it to the ball in your hands.

                When all of the paper has been picked up, throw your ball into the waste basket.

                Accompaniment: "Freeze & Move" (A, 2)

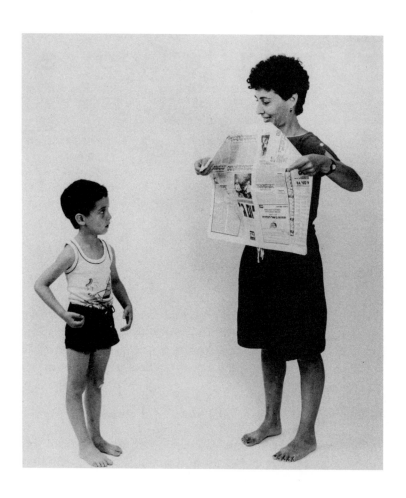

■ Paper Shapes

ADULT &
CHILD

Create a variety of shapes with your newspaper, then copy these shapes with your body.

Place two shapes next to each other so they are touching. Now make those two shapes with your bodies.

Obstacle Course

WHAT YOUR CHILD WILL GAIN FROM THIS EXPERIENCE		

PHYSICAL
Balance
Extending the
  auditory sense
Stimulating the
  nervous system
	COGNITIVE
	Listening skills
	Concentration
		EMOTIONAL/SOCIAL
		Confidence
		Self-esteem
		Fun!

● You Need

Moveable objects such as chairs, pillows, or sponges. Avoid potentially dangerous, sharp-edged, or breakable objects. Scatter the objects throughout the room so that you can walk around them easily.

CHILD Take the adult's hand and close your eyes.

ADULT Walking slowly, lead the child on a path that snakes between and around the objects being careful not to touch them.

CHILD Open your eyes. Now it's your turn to lead the adult.

ADULT & Repeat the same exercise walking backward.
CHILD
The same exercise can be done outdoors: in the yard; in the park; at the beach; etc. In unfamiliar places, only the adult should lead.

Pencil and Paper

WHAT YOUR CHILD WILL GAIN FROM THIS EXPERIENCE		

PHYSICAL
Strong and flexible
  feet & ankles
Balance
Eye-foot coordination
	COGNITIVE
	Problem solving
	Exercising both sides
	  of the brain
		EMOTIONAL/SOCIAL
		Feelings of
		  accomplishment
		Fun!

▲ You Need

A large square sheet of paper, about 18 × 18 inches, and two short pencils.

▲ Foot Drawing

CHILD   Hold a pencil between your toes (any toes). Draw anything you like on the paper. Now try it with the other foot.

▲ Pencil Walk

CHILD   Stand up and put a pencil between the toes of each foot (turn the points downward). Walk on your heels. Keep your toes as high as you can so that you won't leave any marks on the floor.

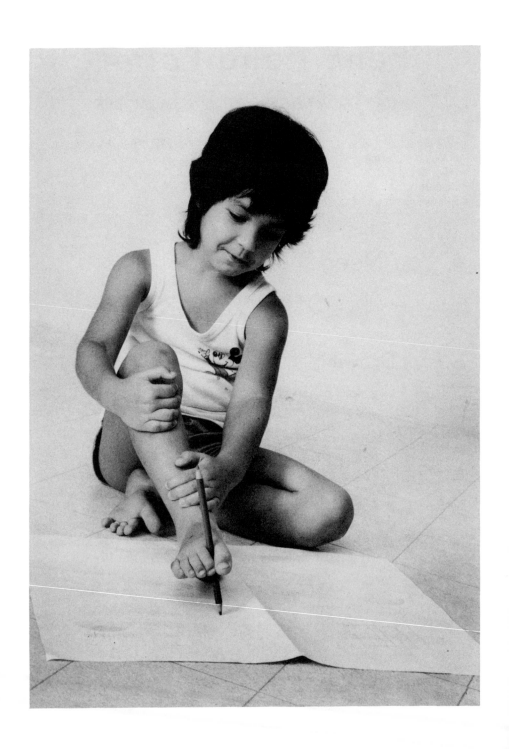

Pillow

■ You Need

A small pillow, not too soft, and bare feet.?

■ Bridge

CHILD   Make a bridge over the pillow with your body. (So your kitten can go across the "puddle" without getting wet.)

You can make a bridge by standing on one side of the pillow and putting your hands down on the floor on the other side. You can stand with one foot on each side of the pillow. Try standing on one foot and putting only one hand down. The other hand and foot are in the air.

How else can you make a bridge?

■ Boat Pillow

CHILD   Place your pillow in the middle of the floor. Pretend that the pillow is a boat, and sit on the boat. Water has come in onto the floor of the boat. You don't want to get your feet wet! Lift both legs and arms high into the air!

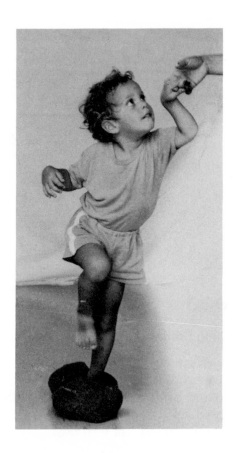

Put your stomach on the pillow. Lift your head, arms, and legs high in the air, so they too can stay out of the water.

Stand on the pillow. Can you lift one leg? Can you lift the other leg? Hold the adult's hand if you need to so you don't fall into the water.

ADULT   Hold the child's hand to provide balance when needed.

■ Mirror

ADULT &   Pretend that the pillow is a mirror that you can
CHILD   see yourself in. Make funny faces at yourself.

■ Pillow Pass

ADULT &
CHILD

Sit down facing each other. Pass the pillow to each other with two hands; one hand and then the other; then your feet. How else can you pass the pillow?

Repeat each of the above while sitting slightly farther apart. You will need to stretch your body in order to reach each other.

Now sit back to back. Pass the pillow to each other overhead with two hands; with one hand and then the other; twisting around to the side; and then to the other side. Can you do it with your feet? How else can you pass the pillow?

Stand up and try to repeat all of the variations that you discovered. Maybe you will discover new ones like tossing the pillow between your legs. What else can you do with the pillow?

■ Puddle

CHILD

Put the pillow on the floor. Pretend the pillow is a puddle, and you must jump over it without getting wet. How can you jump?

Try jumping: with one foot and landing on the other; with the other foot, landing on the same foot; with both feet; and with a turn in the air. How else can you jump over the puddle?

■ Turtle

CHILD

Pretend you are a turtle. Get on your hands and knees. The pillow is your shell. Ask the adult to put your shell onto your back (and to replace it if it falls). Crawl around trying to keep your shell on.

Now the adult is the turtle and you must replace the shell if it falls. Can you replace it using your feet?

Rolling Pin

WHAT YOUR CHILD WILL GAIN FROM THIS EXPERIENCE		
PHYSICAL *Strength & flexibility for feet, arches, & ankles* *Balance* *Stamina*	COGNITIVE *Understanding the laws of motion & gravity* *Motor planning*	EMOTIONAL/SOCIAL *Overcoming fear* *Trust* *Patience*

● You Need

An ordinary household rolling pin and bare feet.

● Balancing Act

CHILD   Place the rolling pin on the floor. Place one of your feet on top of the rolling pin, and press and roll it as though you were rolling-out bread dough. Now give the other foot a turn.

The rolling pin is on the floor in front of you, and the adult is facing you. Hold hands with the adult, and carefully stand on the rolling pin.

● Logroll

ADULT   To perform this activity, the child must feel very confident with standing on the rolling pin. Be patient. The confidence will come with practice and success.

CHILD   Can you travel forward on the rolling pin? How about backward? Move very slowly.

ADULT   Be sure to hold the child's hands, and be careful to step away only when you feel that the child is succeeding, otherwise he or she may be thrown off balance.

Rope

WHAT YOUR CHILD WILL GAIN FROM THIS EXPERIENCE	
PHYSICAL Balance Coordination Agility Strength	EMOTIONAL/SOCIAL Cooperation Trust Confidence Fun!

▲ You Need

A rope about the size and strength of a jump rope without handles (about two yards long); a soft pillow; and a safe place with a comfortable, soft, carpeted floor.

▲ Rope Roll

ADULT Hang the rope on a door knob so that the child can hold both ends. Be sure that the door is closed securely. (You may prefer to put the rope somewhere else: a solid chair; the leg of a piano; etc.)

CHILD Hold each end of the rope in each hand. Lie on your back. Cross one foot over the rope near one hand, cross the other foot near the other hand, and roll on you back from one side to the other.

▲ Rope Swing

ADULT Hang the rope from a strong support. Tie the two ends together firmly to create a swing.

CHILD Sit on the swing. Go forward and back or move from side to side.

Stand on the swing (you may need some help to feel secure).
How else can you ride on the swing? On your stomach? Your back?

▲ Rope Ride

*ADULT &
CHILD*   Hold either end of the rope. Ask the child to sit on the floor, then walk slowly, pulling him or her along.

▲ Pillow Ride

ADULT   Tie one end of the rope onto a small, soft pillow. Pull the child as you did in Rope Ride.

CHILD   Sit on the pillow and take a ride. Now try different ways of riding. Stand on the pillow; lie on your stomach; and lie on your back and grasp the pillow between your legs.

Now it's the adult's turn to sit on the pillow while you pull.

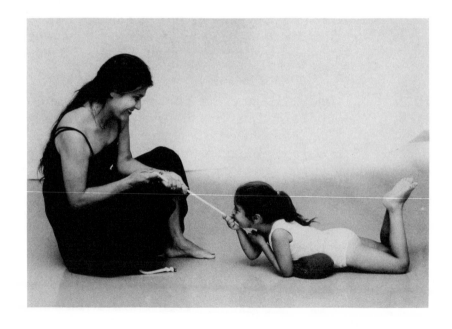

▲ Pillow Chase

CHILD   Hold the rope with the pillow at the other end and walk with it.

                  Run with it, as fast as you can.

ADULT   Follow the pillow wherever it goes.

CHILD   Now it's your turn to chase the pillow while the adult pulls it.

▲ Kangaroo

CHILD   Stand on your pillow. Hold onto the middle of the rope and jump around the room with the pillow, like a kangaroo. Everytime your feet come down, they must land on the pillow.

▲ Freeze & Move for a Group

ADULTS   Each child is holding the end of a rope. The other end is tied around a pillow. The pillow is on the floor.

CHILDREN   When the music plays, run, pulling your pillow behind you. When the music stops, stand on your pillow.

                  This time when the music stops, stand on someone else's pillow while still hanging onto your own rope.

                  Now land on someone else's pillow and hand your rope to the person who is standing on your pillow.

                  Finally, when the music stops, hold your rope and lift someone else's pillow. When the music starts again, dance, holding both your rope and someone else's pillow.

Accompaniment: "Freeze & Move" (A, 2)

Scarves

WHAT YOUR CHILD WILL GAIN FROM THIS EXPERIENCE		

PHYSICAL
Strength
Stamina
Isolating &
  articulating different
  parts of the body
Spatial awarness
Small muscle activity
	COGNITIVE
	Observation skills
	Listening skills
	Motor planning
	Verbal skills
	Concentration
	Aesthetic awareness
	Response to music
	Awareness of space/form
		EMOTIONAL/SOCIAL
		Closer adult-child
		  relationship
		Imagination
		Multicultural experience
		Sensitivity

■ You Need

A soft, translucent scarf for each of you. If possible, find a scarf that will float, rather than fall, when you throw it into the air.

■ Walk the Puppy

ADULT &
CHILD

Hold one corner of your scarf. Pretend that your scarf is a puppy and you are taking your puppy for a walk. Lower your arm so that the scarf is touching the floor and walk slowly. Look down to see whether the puppy is following you and enjoying its walk. Walk backward. Where is your puppy now?

Stand in place and open your legs. Your legs are now a bridge. Let your puppy walk under the bridge.

Stand back to back to each other. Open your legs to make a double bridge. Now exchange puppies.

Accompaniment: "Invisible Strings" (A, 1)

■ Scarf Ball

*ADULT &
CHILD*

Lay your scarf flat on the floor. With your bare feet, step on it carefully without making wrinkles.

Using *only* your feet, make a ball out of the scarf. Then using *only* your feet, make it flat again.

Can you use a different part of your body to make a ball and then make it flat? Try using your nose, shoulder, or elbow. What other body parts can you use?

Using your hands, make a scarf ball and hold it between your ankles. Hold hands and jump. Jump in place, jump forward, jump backward, etc.

Standing at different ends of the room, hold the scarf ball between your ankles. Jump to each other, hug, and exchange scarves. Make a new scarf ball between your ankles and jump backward away from each other.

■ Magic Mirror Scarves

ADULT   Stand facing the child as each of you holds your scarf by one corner. If the child is holding the scarf in the right hand, hold yours in your left hand, so that the scarves appear as they would if you were looking into a mirror. When you move your scarf, be sure that it goes only as high as the child's scarf can reach.

Say to the child: *"Our scarves are magic! They can talk to each other without words! My scarf will tell your scarf which way to move."*

Move your scarf very, very slowly as you encourage the child to imitate your movements.

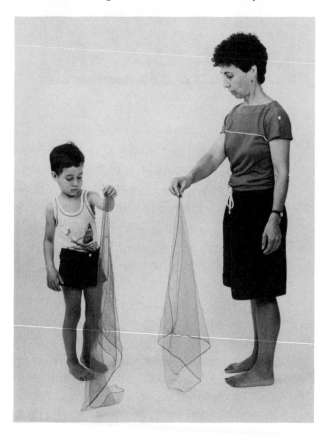

Feel as though your scarf is tied to the child's scarf by some invisible string, so that both scarves are always moving together exactly. Keep the movement very simple. Your aim is to synchronize your movements with the movements of the child.

It is difficult for a very young child to move very slowly because slow motion requires small muscle control. The child must gradually develop strength in these muscles in order to control them. Focusing on the magic, mystery, and drama of the situation and feeling the intense closeness that you are generating by being sure that the scarves are constantly moving together will motivate the child to keep trying. Do not give in to the child's desire to move quickly. Concentration will be short in the first sessions, but be patient. Repeat this game again a week later. You will see improvement with each repetition.

Once the child has mastered following your movements, you can increase the challenge by saying: *"Pretend that we have a red scarf in the other hand. The pretend scarves are also magic. They also talk to each other."*

Move your hand as though you are holding a scarf. Watch closely and feel the child's hand moving with yours. Gradually begin to move both hands at the same time. Move slowly enough so that you are able to observe both of the child's hands.

Accompaniment: "Invisible Strings" (A, 1)

■ Scarf Bridges

ADULT   Hold one scarf in each hand. Open your arms wide, letting the scarf hang toward the floor. You will notice that you have created a space between you and your body, with your arm acting as a kind of bridge.

CHILD   Move and dance under and around the bridges.

ADULT   As the child dances, do slow motion movements
             that create new bridge forms: change your arm
             position, turn your body, change levels, and
             change directions.

■ Freeze & Move

ADULT &   Stand and hold your scarf. When the music is
CHILD   playing, wave your scarf through space as if it
             were dancing. When the music stops, freeze like a
             statue and open your fingers. Watch the scarf
             float to the ground. When the music starts again,
             pick up your scarf and dance with it to the music.

ADULT   Ask the child: *"Did you hear different kinds of
             music? Fast and slow? Scary? Happy? Mexican?
             African? What else did you hear?"*

This time, if the music is slow, bend down *very slowly* to pick up your scarf and dance slowly with it. If the music is fast, bend down and pick it up quickly and dance fast.

Accompaniment: "Freeze & Move" (A, 2)

ADULT   Encourage the child to verbalize the various feelings expressed in the many samples of music. At a very young age, this verbalization is kept at a simple level. When the child is older, this verbal/musical game can become quite sophisticated. You can listen not only for movement qualities or the name of a country, but also for composers, styles, eras, etc.

Moving to the music is a way of listening with your whole body—your whole being—so that you not only hear the music more fully, you connect with it, and it becomes part of you.

■ Variation on Freeze & Move

CHILD   This time, do just the opposite. When the music plays, freeze. When it stops, move.

ADULT   If the older child feels too grownup to use a scarf, just make a game of "statues" out of it.

Sponges

WHAT YOUR CHILD WILL GAIN FROM THIS EXPERIENCE		

PHYSICAL
Full body strength
Flexibility
Balance
Eye-hand & eye-foot
   coordination
Tactile sense
Lateralization
Relaxation
Stamina
	COGNITIVE
	Response to music
	Color awareness
	Exercising both
	   hemispheres of the
	   brain
	Concentration
	Ability to organize
	Academic ability
	Observation skills
	Spatial awareness
	Naming colors
	Naming body parts
	Sculptural forms
		EMOTIONAL/SOCIAL
		Confidence
		Closer adult-child
		   relationship
		Multicultural experience
		Sensitivity
		Fun!

● You Need

Bare feet and at least one ordinary household sponge for each of you. They can be the same shape, but a variety of bright colors is fun. If you have four or five sponges, you will have even more fun.

● Guess What?

ADULT   Use this game to introduce the other sponge games. Make sure the child doesn't see the sponge until the game is under way.

CHILD   Sit with your eyes closed and your hands behind your back. The adult will give you something, but don't look.

ADULT   With great mystery, place the sponge in the child's hands. Ask the child to feel the sponge and try to guess what it is without looking.

Say to the child: *"Open your eyes and look at the sponge. Did you guess what it was? What could you tell about the sponge? Color? Smell? What else?"*

● It's Alive

ADULT &
CHILD

Hold your sponge in one hand. Squeeze it hard, then feel the sponge trying to push your hand away as you slowly let go.

Squeeze the sponge with the other hand and with other parts of your body: between both bare feet; the inside of each elbow; each knee; each armpit; and your neck. Don't forget to feel the sponge pushing you away as you let go. What other parts of your body can you use to squeeze the sponge?

Stand up. Press the top of the sponge first with your whole foot and then with your toes only (give each foot a turn). Try the outside of each foot, the inside of each foot, your big toe on each foot, your little toe on each foot, your toe nails, and each heel.

ADULT

If the child is old enough and seems ready for an additional challenge, try combining some of the above: the toes of one foot with the heel of the other, for example.

● Kick-sponge

ADULT &
CHILD

Place a sponge on top of one foot and kick it to each other. Catch it with your hands. Give each foot a turn.

● Jump-sponge

CHILD

Stand at opposite ends of the room from the adult. Put the sponge between your legs at the knees or ankles. Try to jump toward the adult without dropping the sponge. If you make it, give the sponge to the adult and get a kiss in return. Now it's the adult's turn to jump the sponge to you.

This time, hold one sponge between your legs *and* the other sponge on top of your head. You will need both hands to keep the sponge on your head as you jump. Again jump to the adult.

Accompaniment: "Jumping" (A, 4)

● Animals

CHILD   Standing up, hold one sponge in each hand. Pretend that you are a prehistoric animal and the sponges are great big paws. Keeping your legs straight, place your paws on the ground and take a little walk in the forest.

Get on your hands and knees, and ask the adult to place a sponge on your back. Pretend that you are a turtle with a shell on your back and crawl.

● Tower

CHILD   Place one sponge on top of another. Use as many sponges as you can. If your tower topples, do it again.

Can you lift the tower and then set it back down again?

● What Happened?

CHILD   Using four or five sponges of different colors, place them flat on the floor side by side, so that they form a straight line.

Look at them carefully for a moment, then close your eyes.

ADULT   While the child's eyes are closed, change the position of one of the sponges. For example, if the yellow sponge was at one end of the line, place it at the other end, or place the yellow sponge on *top* of the blue sponge, etc. Make only one very simple change in the beginning of this game.

Say to the child: *"Open your eyes. What happened? Right, this sponge was moved. Where was it before? Do you know the name of that color? Would you like to try it again? Close your eyes."*

ADULT Because movement is the child's natural form of expression, the child will tend to *show* you what changes you made. That's fine. Do not inhibit this natural expression; however, encourage the child to verbalize the action.

Ask the child, *"Can you tell me with words, did I put the yellow sponge behind my back? No? Where did I put it?"* Try to keep the questions light, fun, and humorous, so it doesn't become a test.

As you continue to play the game, the changes can become more and more complex, but only if the child remains avidly interested. When interest begins to lag, it's a sure sign that the child is no longer learning. Return to the game next week.

● Sponge Sculpture

ADULT & CHILD

Place two sponges on the floor so that they are touching each other in some way. You have created a sculptural form with the two sponges.

Leave the sponges where they are for reference and try to make the same shape and the same relationship with your two bodies.

When you are satisfied with your first attempt, make a new form with the sponges and again create the sculpture with your bodies.

Think up new forms and new ways of interpreting them with your bodies.

● Gliding

ADULT &
CHILD

Place a sponge flat on the floor in front of one foot. Inch the sponge forward across the floor, by giving it a little push with your toe as you walk. Try to make it glide in a straight line.

Do the same movement with two sponges using one for each foot.

● Leaping

ADULT

Begin by demonstrating a leap for the child: a leap is a change of weight *in the air* from one leg to another. Stand at one end of the room with your arms open wide and your head high. Now run quickly toward the sponge and leap over it.

Say to the child: *"Now it is your turn. You are a beautiful big bird. Spread your wings very wide. The sponge is a high mountain. Look up at the sky as you fly and then leap over the high mountain."*

This time, hold hands and run and leap together. You will have to place the sponges carefully so that you each reach your sponge at the same time. You will also have to adjust the size and speed of your running step and the height of your leap to that of the child. Be sensitive to the child's needs and abilities. Enjoy the exhilaration of running together and "flying" into the air together.

When you have had enough practice, leap together *without* holding hands. The challenge is to be so kinesthetically aware and sensitive to each other that you are both in the air at exactly the same time. This may take a lot of practice but it is well worth the effort. You will both feel wonderful and very, very close.

Accompaniment: "Leaping" (A, 5)

● Leaping Variation

ADULT   Place two sponge mountains in a line. Space them just far enough apart so that you can do two leaps, one after another, using alternate legs. After your demonstration, shorten the distance between the sponges, to adjust to the size of the child's legs.

CHILD   Now you must leap over two mountains. Be sure to give each leg a turn.

ADULT   This is an extremely important development. The young child has had little experience with leading out and landing on the weaker leg (we all have a stronger side). Be patient and kind, but persistent. Hold the child's hand if she or he needs help. Making both sides of the body equally skillful will affect the way in which the brain develops.

● Balancing Act

ADULT &
CHILD   Place your sponges on top of your head and walk slowly around the room balancing them. Enjoy the quiet peaceful feeling of moving in slow motion.

Now walk backwards, gradually add movement in the arms, try a very slow turn, or changing levels. Experiment with slow motion movements on the floor while balancing the sponge.

Continue to improvise, but now try placing the sponge on different parts of the body: the back of your outstretched hand; your shoulder; or your back. Can you close your eyes and balance the sponge while moving in place?

Accompaniment: "Invisible Strings" (A, 1)

● Magic Walk

ADULT	Place as many sponges as you have in a random pattern on the floor.
	Say to the child: *"Do you see all of those sponges? We're going to make magic. You're going to walk all around the room and you won't step on any of the sponges—even with your eyes closed! Now, close your eyes and take my hand."*
	Walk the child very slowly—and mysteriously—between and around the sponges. Be sure that neither one of you steps on them.
CHILD	Now it's your turn to lead the adult.

● Freeze & Move

ADULT &
CHILD

Place as many sponges as you have in a random pattern on the floor.

When the music plays, dance around the room without touching the sponges. When the music stops, jump onto the nearest sponge with both feet and freeze into a statue until the music starts again.

Try some fun variations: When the music stops, land on only one foot; touch only your elbow to the sponge; touch only your head, your nose, your ear, or next time, sit on the sponge.

Have fun thinking up variations.

Accompaniment: "Freeze & Move" (A, 2)

● Basket-Sponge

ADULT

Play this game when the other activities with sponges are over and you would like to gather them up.

Hold a large plastic bag (or any other container with a really wide opening) low enough for the child to throw the sponges into. Adjust the distance to the child's abilities.

Stuffed Animals

▲ You Need

A medium sized, favorite stuffed animal.

▲ Friends

ADULT & CHILD

Each of you hold one of the animal's hands. With the animal between you, take a little walk.

Walk forward, backward, sideways, and in a circle. Try swinging the animal between you, or running and jumping with the animal.

▲ Choo-Choo Train

ADULT

Say to the child: *"Pretend that you are a choo-choo train and that your animal is your engineer. Hold your animal out in front of you and carefully move around the room. Engineers are always careful to watch where they are going so that they won't have an accident."*

Stand behind the child with your hands on his or her shoulders. Set the child's pace by periodically

calling out, *"red light!,"* then, *"green light!"* Also call out, *"tunnel!"* occasionally, at which point you will both bend low while continuing to move.

CHILD Now it's your turn to be the caboose. Your animal can be in the middle or can still be the engineer. Don't forget to say, *"red light!"* especially if the adult is heading towards a danger zone.

Accompaniment: "Choo-choo Train" (A, 5)

▲ Cuddling

CHILD Touch your nose to the animal's nose, ear, head, toe, back, etc.

ADULT Suggest as many parts as you notice on the animal.

ADULT & Now play the cuddling game with each other
CHILD instead of with the animal. Touch noses, ears, heads, toes, backs, etc.

▲ Cradle

ADULT Say to the child: *"Pretend your animal is a baby. Hold your baby in your lap, and sit in my lap. Listen to the music, and rock back and forth. If you feel like it, close your eyes, and ask your baby to close his or her eyes too."*

Accompaniment: "Invisible Strings" (A, 1)

▲ Rowboat

ADULT & Sit on the floor facing each other, and open your
CHILD legs wide. The adult's legs will open much wider than the child's, so place the child's feet inside of the adult's open legs so that they touch at about the knees.

Place the animal on the floor between you. Take both hands with each other. Smile. Pretend that you are a rowboat, carrying the animal across the river. Still holding hands, one of you lies backward toward the floor, then the other tries to lie back. Move slowly back and forth, giving the animal a ride, while you get a good leg stretch.

▲ Slide

CHILD Sit down. Put your hands on the floor behind you. Lift your feet off the floor. Ask the adult to put the stuffed animal onto your feet. Pretend that the animal is on a slide. Lift your feet and let it slide down into your lap. Ask the adult to put the animal on your feet again, so you can repeat the exercise.

This time, lift your feet suddenly, making the animal fly over your head. See if the adult can catch it.

PART TWO:
Using the Imagination

Backward Walks & Runs

WHAT YOUR CHILD WILL GAIN FROM THIS EXPERIENCE		
PHYSICAL	COGNITIVE	EMOTIONAL/SOCIAL
Balance	Problem solving	Confidence
Coordination	Measuring distance	Trust
Peripheral vision		Fun!
Auditory development		
Spatial awareness		

▲ You Need

A large room free of obstacles.

ADULT

Kneel a short distance from the child with your arms open wide. Instruct the child to walk backwards toward you. When she or he arrives, wrap your arms around the child with a hug.

Say to the child: *"This is a game. See if you can walk to me backwards without looking! You don't have to be afraid because I will catch you. You will hear me talking to you so you will know which way to go. Ready? Go!"*

The child will need for you to be speaking almost constantly to feel sure that you are there. Say things like: *"I'm here. I'm waiting for you"; "I'll catch you. I love you";* or *"I'm waiting to hug you."*

In the beginning, it can be quite frightening to move into unknown space. Be reassuring. Keep the spirit of fun and play and joy in your voice. Accentuate the positive with expressions like, *"That was great! I'm sure that next time you won't have to look at all!"* Repeat only twice on the first day, then try another exercise. You'll find that when you return to this one a few days later, the child will already show an increase in confidence. Eventually, as the child gains confidence, extend the distance between you. When the child is ready, substitute a run for the walk.

Accompaniment: "Choo-choo Train" (A, 5)

Bridges and Snakes

WHAT YOUR CHILD WILL GAIN FROM THIS EXPERIENCE		
PHYSICAL	COGNITIVE	EMOTIONAL/SOCIAL
Strength	Problem solving	Self-esteem
Flexibility	Directional awareness	Feelings of
Balance	Structural awareness	accomplishment
Spatial awareness	Imgination	Joy!

■ You Need

A clean, spacious floor area and the furniture that is already in the room.

ADULT — Create a bridge with your body by standing on both feet and placing both hands on the floor. Your arms and legs are opened wide.

CHILD — You are a snake crawling under the bridge. Lie on your stomach and wiggle your body until you pass under the bridge. Stretch your arms and legs very long.

ADULT — Try varying the space between your arms and legs to create different kinds of bridges. You can also use the furniture to invent new bridges. Put one foot on the sofa, or both hands on a chair, and so on. Have fun with various objects and body positions.

Encourage the child to thoroughly explore each position before you change.

CHILD — This time pretend you are a choo-choo train riding through a tunnel.

What else can go under bridges or through tunnels? Try making up some games of your own.

Close and Open: Jackknife

WHAT YOUR CHILD WILL GAIN FROM THIS EXPERIENCE	
PHYSICAL *Back strength* *Stomach muscle strength* *Coordination* *Flexibility* *Tactile sense* *Full body stretch* *Neck stretch*	EMOTIONAL/SOCIAL *Interdependence* *Closer adult-child relationship*

● You Need

A smooth, clean floor.

ADULT &
CHILD

Lie down on the floor, close to each other. Stretch your arms and legs and roll onto your right side. The child's back is touching the adult's stomach. Th back of the child's legs are touching the adult's legs.

Together, bring your hands and feet toward each other while keeping your legs straight. You are closing up like a jackknife or a clam.

Slowly open, keeping your knees straight, and return to the original position.

Repeat about four times, then turn onto your left side and repeat four times. This exercise will make you both feel cozy.

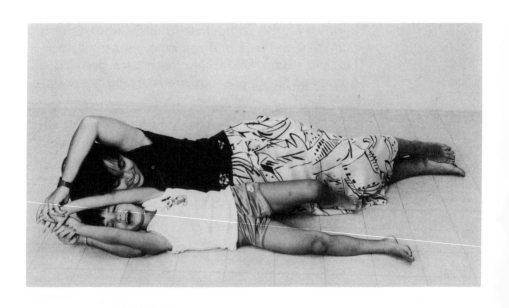

Prehistoric Animal

WHAT YOUR CHILD WILL GAIN FROM THIS EXPERIENCE		
PHYSICAL Stretching: hamstrings; calf; achilles tendon; spinal column; and neck. Kinesthetic sense Blood circulation Relaxation	COGNITIVE Directional awareness Academic ability Concentration	EMOTIONAL/SOCIAL Closer adult-child relationship Release of tension Recalling the fun of crawling Fun!

▲ You Need

A clean floor and a spacious area.

ADULT
Say to the child as you demonstrate: *"I am a great, big prehistoric animal. I am walking on all fours. My heels are on the floor, and my hands are flat on the floor. I'm also trying to keep my knees straight. That isn't easy, but if I keep trying, my legs will get stretched and I will get tall and strong. My head is down too, so I can see you and smile at you when you crawl after me."*

CHILD
Get on your hands and knees, and peek at the adult's face between your legs. Smile at the adult, and crawl forward as the prehistoric animal goes for a walk. Remind the adult to smile.

Now it's your turn to be the prehistoric animal. Remember to try to keep your whole foot and hand on the floor and your knees straight while walking. Also remember to smile at the adult.

ADULT
If you can crawl, fine. If that is too hard on your knees, the child will understand. Just bend over so

that you can see the child's face and wave and smile. The smiling at each other motivates the child to look down. Lowering the head stretches the entire body, all the way from head to heels.

If the child is having difficulty with keeping the heels on the floor or keeping the knees straight, don't make an issue of it. She or he may still be too young to handle all of the elements at once. In due time, it will happen.

Do not repeat this exercise more than twice across the floor in any one session, or you may strain your backs.

Rolling Log

WHAT YOUR CHILD WILL GAIN FROM THIS EXPERIENCE		
PHYSICAL Body awareness Full body stretch Strength: pelvic area Directional awareness Coordination Relaxation	COGNITIVE Motor planning Concentration Ability to organize Ability to visualize Imagination	EMOTIONAL/SOCIAL Relaxation Trust Closer adult-child relationship Fun!

● You Need

A clean, smooth floor.

CHILD Pretend that you are a very tall tree that was just cut down by a logger. Lie down at one end of the room. You are now a log. Stretch your arms over your head to make yourself very long. Straighten your knees and lengthen your toes to make your legs very long.

ADULT You are the logger. You are holding an imaginery pole: the kind that loggers use to nudge logs from rocks, as they roll down mountain rivers.

The pole is long, so you don't need to bend over to push the log.

Say to the child: *"Watch my pole and feel it pushing you down the river."*

CHILD Roll very, very slowly towards the other side of the room. Try to keep your arms stretched, your knees straight, and your toes and fingers long. If you move very slowly with your whole body stretched long, you will make a perfectly straight line across the room. Feel the pole pushing you.

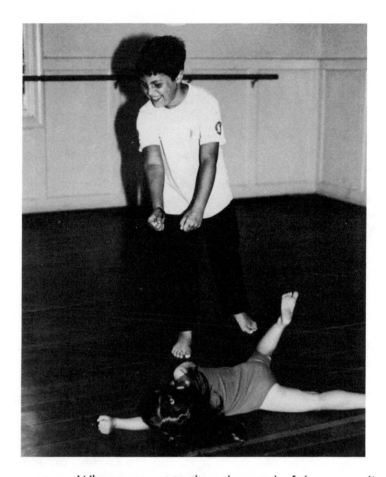

When you get to the other end of the room, lie on your back. Relax and wait for the adult to put down the pole.

ADULT   Take the child's hands or feet and drag the log to the truck that's waiting to take it to the lumber yard.

Be sure that the child is on his or her back; you have a choice of holding the child's wrists or ankles. You might want to try to see which is more comfortable (or more fun) for the child. Encourage the child to relax.

Sensing: Am I Close?

WHAT YOUR CHILD WILL GAIN FROM THIS EXPERIENCE		
PHYSICAL *Extending all of the senses* *Directional awareness* *Relaxation*	COGNITIVE *Listening skills* *Concentration*	EMOTIONAL/SOCIAL *Closer adult/child relationship* *Sensitivity*

■ You Need

A time and place when the child can be as comfortable and relaxed as possible. Just after reading a quiet story together or as the child is waking from a nap are both good times.

CHILD
Lie down somewhere where you can be comfortable and close your eyes.

ADULT
Slowly and quietly, say to the child: *"While you lie there with your eyes closed, I will walk around the room as quietly as I can. Sometimes I will be coming closer to you, sometimes I will be walking away. When I stop talking, you won't hear my voice any more. Try to feel when I am coming closer to you. When you feel me coming close, lift one hand. When you feel me going away, put your hand down. Don't forget to keep your eyes closed."*

Move carefully around the room approaching the child from a variety of directions. Do not get anxious if the child succeeds only part of the time. These senses require exercising. Just repeat the game from time to time, and your patience will be rewarded.

There are any number of possible ways that the child will sense your closeness: sound vibrations; shadows; floor vibrations; and through senses for which we have no name.

CHILD   Now it's your turn to walk around while the adult is lying down with eyes closed. Be sure to walk slowly and quietly.

Sliding

WHAT YOUR CHILD WILL GAIN FROM THIS EXPERIENCE		

PHYSICAL
Coordination
Spatial awareness
Directional awareness
Lateralization
Strength in legs
	COGNITIVE
	Academic ability
	Specialization of each
	  side of body & brain
	Motor planning
	Responding to music
		EMOTIONAL/SOCIAL
		Closer adult-child
		  relationship
		Fun!

▲ You Need

A smooth floor.

ADULT &
CHILD

Face each other and hold hands.

With your right foot, step to the side. Ask the child to imitate you by stepping with the left foot to the left. You are both travelling in the same direction.

As you draw your left foot to your right foot, make a sliding sound on the floor.

Repeat the movement a few times until it flows smoothly. Then do it to the other side until you feel ready to dance it with the music.

Make your steps small enough to match the steps of the child. Do not pull on the child's arms; allow the strength to develop in the child's legs.

Once you are having fun dancing together, the child may lose the skill developed during the practice session. This is natural. Because one leg is always stronger than the other, the child may want to cross the weaker leg over the stronger one instead of sliding it on the floor. Be patient, but persistant. The correction can often be made quite easily by reminding the child, *"Let me hear your slide."*

It has been proven that brain development is enhanced when both sides of the body are functioning skillfully.

Accompaniment: "Sliding" (A, 6)

Somersaults

WHAT YOUR CHILD WILL GAIN FROM THIS EXPERIENCE	
PHYSICAL Stretch and flexibility for the back Suppleness Coordination Strength in arms & shoulders	EMOTIONAL/SOCIAL Confidence Trust Fun!

● You Need

A soft rug or mat or even a thick towel that is at least as long as the child's body.

ADULT   When a somersault is done correctly, it is sheer pleasure and fun, but when done incorrectly, it can cause injury and give the child a fright. Often, when young children try to somersault by themselves, they put their heads on the floor and throw their legs into the air. They are balanced for a few seconds on the top of their heads, then they flop over flat on their backs. That flop can be a shock to the child's spine.

A somersault is a kind of status symbol for children. If their friends can do it and they can't they feel inadequate. Both the frightened child and the child who has not yet tried it will be grateful to you if you teach it to them correctly.

● Front Somersault

ADULT   Stand the child at one end of the rug, with feet slightly apart.

Say to the child: *"Bend down and put this part of your head on the rug."* Gently place your hand on

the back of the child's head, close to the back of the neck. The child will naturally bend the knees in order to get low enough.

With one of your hands, tuck the child's head far enough so that the back of the neck touches the rug. With your other hand on the child's buttocks, you can gently flip the child. The rounded back will smoothly roll into a somersault.

CHILD   Now that you know how to do a somersault, try it by yourself. Be careful to tuck your head way under. If you are on a big rug, practice somersaulting from one end of the room to the other.

● Back Somersault

ADULT   The child is lying flat on his or her back on the mat or rug.

Place the child's hands overhead with bent elbows pointing to the ceiling. The hands are flat on the floor near the shoulders. Gently encourage the child's fingers to straighten.

Stand near the child's head.

Say to the child: *"Try to press your hands against the floor as you swing your legs up to me."*

Catch the child's feet with both hands and lift the child's body up toward the ceiling. Remind the child to, *"Push the floor with your hands."* The child's body is vertical, poised for a moment in a handstand. She or he is supporting the body on the hands, while you are holding the feet.

Allow the child's knees to bend as you place the child's feet onto the floor to complete the somersault. The child is now standing.

The child should be at least four years old before you try this movement. A good bit of strength in the arm and shoulder muscles is required to accomplish a back somersault. Unless your child is already five years old, do not expect her or him to do a back somersault without your assistance. Continue to help the child and you will gradually see the strength developing in the arm and shoulder muscles as you encourage with, *"Push the floor hard with your hands."* When you see that the child is indeed pushing and thereby lifting his or her own weight into the air, the time has come for the child to try it alone.

Swinging

WHAT YOUR CHILD WILL GAIN FROM THIS EXPERIENCE		
PHYSICAL
Relaxation
Coordination	COGNITIVE
Specialization of each
side of the body &
brain
Awareness of
gravitational force
Motor planning	EMOTIONAL/SOCIAL
Closer adult/child
relationship
Sensitivity
Fun!

■ You Need

Space enough for your arms to swing freely without bumping into anything.

*ADULT &
CHILD*
Imagine that your arm is a swing, the kind that you see at the playground. Swing your arm back and forth and side to side. Now swing the other arm.

Can you swing other parts of your body? Try swinging your head. Try swinging your leg (hold onto a table or chair to help you with your balance). Now try the other leg.

Sit on a high chair and swing your legs back and forth from the knees down.

ADULT
When each of you has explored all of the possibilities within your own bodies, try a variety of swings with each other. Hold one hand and swing together, hold the other hand, and try holding two hands.

Find ways of holding hands and swinging while walking, jumping, and dancing. What else can you do while swinging?

Twirling: Spinning Top

WHAT YOUR CHILD WILL GAIN FROM THIS EXPERIENCE		

PHYSICAL
Balance
Coordination
Directional awareness
Spatial awareness
Arm awareness &
  strength
	COGNITIVE
	Specialization of each
	  side of the body and
	  brain
	Motor planning
	Measuring space
		EMOTIONAL/SOCIAL
		Confidence
		Closer adult-child
		  relationship
		Expressing love
		Joy of movement

▲ You Need

Space enough to twirl freely across the room, with your arms wide apart, and two scarves.

ADULT   Kneel at one end of the room. Open your arms wide and smile to welcome the child.

CHILD   Stand at the other end of the room, open your arms wide, look at the adult, and smile. With tiny, fast, tip-toe steps, twirl yourself around and around like a spinning top. Keep smiling and look at the adult until you reach his or her arms.

ADULT   When the child arrives, give her or him a big hug. Hold the child gently for a while until the dizziness subsides.

If the child is very young, she or he may be frightened to try this exercise. Make it easier by shortening the distance between you. At first, be so close that one turn results in a hug. Then gradually, as the child's confidence grows, increase the space between you.

CHILD   Be a spinning top again, but this time, twirl the
               other way.

ADULT   Have the child hold a scarf by one corner in each
               hand. The child's arm's are still outstretched, so
               that when she or he is twirling, the scarves are
               flying! The child will be thrilled to watch this
               happening, and at the same time, will be
               coordinating many skills at the same time:
               awareness of where the arms are in space;
               awareness of the distance to the adult; and
               awareness of the need to be centered for
               balance.

               Accompaniment: "Twirling" (A, 3)

PART THREE:
Dance-Stories and Rhythmic Chants

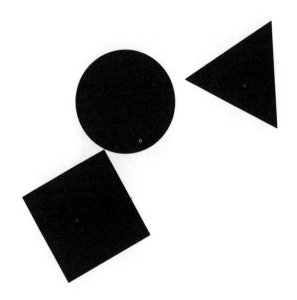

Balloon Dance/Story

WHAT YOUR CHILD WILL GAIN FROM THIS EXPERIENCE		
PHYSICAL *Coordination* *Kinesthetic awareness* *Directional awareness*	COGNITIVE *Response to music* *Knowledge of relative* *size shapes* *Motor planning* *Ability to organize* *Concentration* *Awareness of sculptural* *forms*	EMOTIONAL/SOCIAL *Imagination* *Structure and form* *Freedom of expression* *Closer adult-child* *relationship*

● You Need

Enough space to move freely around the room.

CHILD

How does a balloon look when it has no air in it? Lie down on the floor, and pretend that you are a deflated balloon. The adult will blow you up. Show the adult how a balloon feels and looks when it gets a little bit of air in it, then a little bit more, then a little bit more. You will grow bigger, wider, and taller.

ADULT

Pretend to be blowing up the balloon. Watch the child respond to each of your breaths, and encourage the child with comments like: *"Oh look at that beautiful balloon shape!"; "The balloon is really getting bigger!"; "Your arms are part of the balloon!"; "Your eyes are part of the balloon!"*

When the child's whole body is involved and is as extended and open as possible, put the music on.

CHILD

You are all blown up, and the wind is blowing you all over the sky. Dance with your arms; dance with your head; and dance with your legs.

Suddenly, there's a tiny hole in the balloon. Air begins to seep out. You try to keep dancing, but you are getting smaller . . . and smaller . . . and smaller . . . until finally, there's no more air.

ADULT   Pretend to put a patch on the balloon.

CHILD   Lie very still so that the patch has a chance to dry.

ADULT   Again, blow up the balloon. Encourage the child to make interesting sculptural forms with comments like: *"Remember those beautiful balloon shapes you made before? Try to make them again."*

CHILD   The adult is blowing up the balloon again. You're getting bigger . . . and bigger . . . and bigger.

You are all blown up. The wind is blowing you again. You're floating all over the sky. The wind is getting stronger. You are dancing faster . . . and faster . . . and faster.

Suddenly, the patch falls off! S-s-s-s-s-s-s-s. No more air.

Accompaniment: "Balloon Dance/Story" (B, 1)

Bird in the Nest

WHAT YOUR CHILD WILL GAIN FROM THIS EXPERIENCE		

PHYSICAL
Relaxation
Strength in arms &
  shoulders
Fluidity in arm
  movements
	COGNITIVE
	Motor planning
	Listening skills
		EMOTIONAL/SOCIAL
		Connecting with nature
		The joys of
		  independence
		  and dependence
		Expressing love
		Touching
		Fun!

■ You Need

Enough space to fly around the room freely.

ADULT
: Sit on the floor with the child on your lap. Sit so that you can both be comfortable as you rock side to side. You may be more comfortable on a cushion or even in a rocking chair.

CHILD
: Pretend that you are a baby bird and that the adult is your mama or papa. You are both in a cozy, warm nest high up in a tree, and the wind is blowing the nest gently. It feels good to be rocking together, but after a while, you notice that the wind is getting stronger and stronger.

Suddenly, the nest turns over and you fly out! Flap your wings really hard to stay in the air. Fly around the whole room saying, *"Tweet-tweet, tweet-tweet, tweet-tweet,"* until the adult comes for you.

ADULT
: You are very busy getting the nest back in order, and you are agitated and worried about your little one. Finally, the music changes, and you bring the baby bird back to the nest.

102

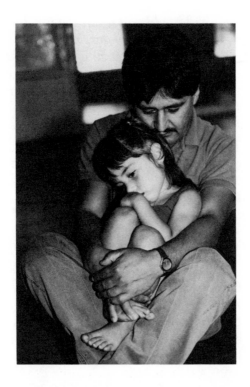

Cuddle back into your rocking movements, and
say to the baby bird: *"I'm so sorry. I apologize.
That was not a very good babysitting job. I'll have to
be more careful the next time. Mama bird (or Papa
bird) loves her baby bird so much. I will protect you.
I hope the wind doesn't get too strong again. Oh-oh,
it's getting stronger."*

CHILD   Again, the nest turns over! Fly around flapping
           your wings, saying, *"Tweet-tweet, tweet-tweet,
           tweet-tweet."* Flap really hard so that your wings
           will get strong.

ADULT   Again, after you busy yourself hurriedly trying to
           fix up the nest, bring your baby back to the nest.

           Return to the rocking movements with the child.
           As you rock say, *"Oh I'm so sorry. I was so worried
           about you. I didn't know if your wings were strong*

enough to hold you up in the air, but it seems that you are getting stronger. You know, this is how baby birds really learn to fly. They keep flapping their wings and practice and practice until their wings get very strong. I'm sure that the next time the nest turns over, your wings will be so strong! Listen for the change in the music. There it is! Now fly!"

This time, do not fuss with the nest. Stand and admire the grown-up bird saying encouraging things like, *"Look at how beautifully my baby bird is flying"; Make your wings long and wide"; They look so strong";* etc.

CHILD   You really know how to fly now, and you know how to go back to the nest all by yourself.

Once you return to the nest, you are very hungry from doing all of that exercise. Your mama (or papa) has food for you. How does a baby bird eat? Yes, from the mama's (or papa's) beak. Nibble, nibble. It's like getting a kiss.

ADULT   Hold, rock, and feed your baby bird. You are both very happy and very proud.

■ Bird in the Nest for a Group

Children love to do this story in groups. They will find many variations on their own. Here are a few suggestions:

All of the children are baby birds in one nest. The adult is babysitting while the parents are out looking for food.

Each child works with a partner. One child is the bird, the other is the mother or father.

All of the children are together in one nest. Different children take turns playing the parts of the adults.

Accompaniment: "Bird in the Nest" (B, 2)

Chay Chay Koolay:
A Movment Song from Ghana, Africa

WHAT YOUR CHILD WILL GAIN FROM THIS EXPERIENCE		
PHYSICAL Locating & articulating parts of the body An experience in rhythm	COGNITIVE Kinesthetic experience of the structure of a song Learning to sing & understand another language Naming parts of the body Using both hemispheres of the brain	EMOTIONAL/SOCIAL Experiencing another culture Closer adult-child relationship

▲ You Need

Only enough space around yourself to move freely. The movements are done standing in one place.

Song

Hands on your head
  (Hands on your head)
Hands on your shoulders
  (Hands on your shoulders)
Hands on your waist
  (Hands on your waist)
Hands on your knees
  (Hands on your knees)
Hands on your ankles
  (Hands on your ankles)
Hands on your ankles
Hey!

Chay chay koo-lay
  (Chay chay koo-lay)
Chay chay ko-fees na
  (Chay chay ko-fees na)
Ko-feesa lahn-ga
  (Ko-feesa lahn-ga)
Kay-tay chee lahn-ga
  (Kay-tay chee lahn-ga)
Koom a dayn-day
  (Koom a dayn-day)
Koom a dayn-day
Hey!

ADULT & *CHILD*	The adult speaks and moves first; the child repeats the words and imitates the movements. This old African form is called "call and echo."

Continue to call and echo until the very last body part is named: the ankles. After each of you has had your turn touching and saying, *"Hands on your ankles,"* remain bent over, touching your ankles and repeat the same line together: *"Hands on your ankles."*

On the word, *"Hey!"* straighten your bodies, stand tall, and clap your hands as though you were playing cymbals. One hand lands high overhead, the other down at your side.

Accompaniment: "Chay Chay Koolay" (B, 3)

Hello Toes

<table>
<tr><td colspan="3">WHAT YOUR CHILD WILL GAIN FROM THIS EXPERIENCE</td></tr>
<tr><td>PHYSICAL</td><td>COGNITIVE</td><td>EMOTIONAL/SOCIAL</td></tr>
<tr><td>Locating & exercising many parts of the body
Exploring new ways of using the body
Feeling rhythm through the body</td><td>Naming many body parts
Integrating the activity of both hemispheres of the brain
Imagination</td><td>Expressing emotions through the body
Closer adult-child relationship
Confidence</td></tr>
</table>

● You Need

Enough space to move freely and a clean floor.

ADULT The act of simultaneously naming a body part, chanting in rhythm, and moving accurately in response to the words and rhythm is a process that integrates the two hemispheres of the brain. Both hemispheres must be functioning harmoniously to make these three activities possible. The constant repetition of this process will result in a smooth and natural flow between thought and action. All hesitation, awkwardness, and clumsiness will disappear.

ADULT & Sit on the floor with your legs stretched out in
CHILD front of you. Chant the words and do the corresponding movement at the same time and in the same rhythm.

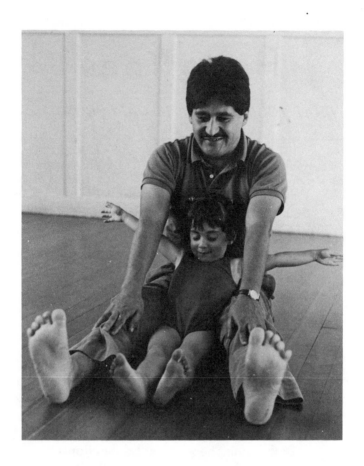

● **Chant**

"Hello Toes"

"Goodbye Toes"

"Hello Toes"

"Goodbye Toes"

"Hello Toes"

● **Movement**

Briskly flex your feet from your ankles so that your toes are pointing toward the ceiling.

Briskly point your toes toward the floor.

Flex.

Point.

Flex.

"My toes are feeling shy"	Slowly and cautiously turn your toes inward toward each other and place the toes on one foot on top of the toes of the other foot protectively.
"And now they feel better"	Return your feet to a natural, relaxed position.
"Hello Hands"	Briskly stretch both arms out in front of you. Your palms are turned upward, facing the ceiling.
"Goodbye Hands"	Briskly bring both arms behind your back, as though hiding your hands.
"Hello Hands"	Move your hands to the front.
"Goodbye Hands"	Move your hands to the back.
"Hello Hands"	Move your hands to the front.
"My hands are feeling shy"	Slowly and cautiously leave the arms outstretched in front of you. Turn both hands inward toward each other with your palms facing downward. Place one hand on top of the other hand protectively.
"And now they feel better"	Smile. Turn your palms upward and reach both arms forward. Lift your head confidently.
"Hello Shoulders"	Briskly lift both shoulders up toward your ears.
"Goodbye Shoulders"	Briskly drop both shoulders down.
"My shoulders are feeling shy"	Slowly and cautiously bring both shoulders toward each other, letting the chest cave in slightly. Allow the head to drop shyly, to one side.

"And now they feel better"	Replace your shoulders to a natural downward position.
	Lift your head confidently. Smile.
"Hello Knees"	Briskly bend your knees and hug them.
"Goodbye Knees"	Briskly straighten your legs again.
"My knees are feeling shy"	Slowly and cautiously turn both knees inward so they seem to be comforting each other. By now, your entire body—your chest, shoulders, and head—are all expressing the feeling of shyness.
"And now they feel better"	Stretch both the legs and arms. Turn your palms upward and lift your head and smile.
ADULT & CHILD	Now you can make up your own movements with different parts of your body. Can you make your elbows shy? Your back? Tongue? Eyes? What else?
	You can also express other feelings: *"My stomach is feeling scared"; "My eyes are feeling sad"; "My whole body is feeling angry"*; etc.
ADULT	When children learn that their feelings exist within their bodies; that they have the power to express them; and that they can make themselves feel better, they are becoming masters over their own lives.
	Accompaniment: "Hello Toes" (B, 4)

Shoo Lie Loo:
An Afro-American
Folk Song

WHAT YOUR CHILD WILL GAIN FROM THIS EXPERIENCE		
PHYSICAL	COGNITIVE	EMOTIONAL/SOCIAL
Locating & articulating parts of the body	Naming parts of the body	Cultural experience
An experience in rhythm	Self-discipline	Closer adult-child relationship
Movement improvisation		Fun!

■ You Need

Enough cleared space to move around the room freely.

Basic Verse

Just from the kitchen
> *Shoo Lie Loo*
With a handful of biscuits
> *Shoo Lie Loo*
Oh Miss Mary
> *Shoo Lie Loo*
Fly away over yonder
> *Shoo Lie Loo*

ADULT & CHILD   The song repeats itself with slight variations in the words. After a while, feel free to make up your own words.

Listen to the song. Clap your hands on the words *"Shoo Lie Loo"* only (three claps). Repeat about four times.

Instead of a clap, move your head on the words *"Shoo Lie Loo"* (three sharp head movements). When your head is not moving, freeze your whole body like a statue. Try to find new ways to move your head each time that you hear *"Shoo Lie Loo."*

Now move only your shoulders on *"Shoe Lie Loo."* Freeze in between, move sharply. Try moving one at a time, then both together. Move them forward and back.

Move only your feet on *"Shoo Lie Loo."* Experiment with how many ways you can move your feet without the rest of your body. Try at least four different variations.

Move your legs only on *"Shoo Lie Loo."* Give each leg a turn. Get on the floor and move both legs at the same time.

Move only your back on *"Shoo Lie Loo."*

Now the whole body moves. Three large, sharp, strong movements using your arms, legs, head, shoulders, back, hips, everything! Freeze right after you do *"Shoo Lie Loo."*

Everything moves again, but now make the movement travel in space. Be sure to freeze in between.

ADULT

This movement song is a lot easier to do than it is to read about. You'll find that if you read the instructions once through while listening to the song, you'll get the gist of it. It's a very simple form and oh, so much fun!

If you are lucky enough to have a tape deck in your car, you'll find that your child will be busy for a long time moving to the song. Even within the confines of a seat belt, the child can move head, hands, shoulders, face, mouth, eyes, nose, chest, and feet.

Accompaniment: "Shoo Lie Loo" (B, 5)

Quiet Time:
"Do You Love Me?"

ADULT   This simple exercise can be performed anytime, anywhere. Do it often with your child. Before bedtime is especially nice.

CHILD   "Do you love me?"

ADULT   "I love your eyes."

"I love your nose."

I love your mouth."

"I love your ears."

(Mention as many parts as you like.)

"What do you think? Do I love you?"

If the child would like to repeat the game and you feel comfortable about the idea, add a light touch to each of the body parts that you name.

Accompaniment: "Sleep Songs" (B, 6)

SPECIAL OFFER
"Hello Toes!" Cassette and Other Dance Books

The authors have prepared a special cassette tape to accompany many of the dance games in Hello Toes! The tape includes folk, classical, and world musics that will increase your enjoyment of the book. To order, fill out the order form on the back of this page.

The Hello Toes! Cassette includes: Invisible Strings; Freeze & Move; Twirling; Jumping; Choo-choo Train; Sliding; Balloon Dance/Story; Bird in the Nest; Chay-Chay Koolay; Hello Toes; Shoo Lie Loo; Sleep Songs. **Price: $10.00**

We also recommend the following titles:

Towards Ballet: Dance Training for the Very Young by Beryl Manthorp. Dance games for children aged 2–5 years that develop posture, coordination, and movement control.   **Price: $10.95**

First Steps in Ballet by Thalia Mara. Beginning ballet exercises at the barre for students age 7 and up.   **Price: $6.95**

The Language of Ballet: A Dictionary by Thalia Mara. Basic terms and famous dancers and choreographers, written for children age 10 and up.   **Price: $9.95**

Ballet: From the First Plié to Mastery by Anna Paskevska. A complete syllabus for the young dancer.   **Price: $19.95**

To order, or to be added to our mailing list, please fill out the form on the back of this page.

ORDER FORM

Please send me:

☐ The Hello Toes! Cassette $10.00

☐ Towards Ballet: Dance Training for the Very Young
by Beryl Manthorp $10.95

☐ First Steps in Ballet by Thalia Mara $6.95

☐ The Language of Ballet: A Dictionary by Thalia Mara $9.95

☐ Ballet: From the First Plié to Mastery, An 8-Year Course
by Anna Paskevska $19.95

Name _____

Address _____

City _____ State _____ Zip _____

Day Phone _____

☐ My check or money order for $ _____ is enclosed.

☐ Please charge my: ☐ Visa   ☐ MasterCard   ☐ American Express

Account Number _____ Exp Date _____

Signature _____

☐ Please send your FREE dance book and video catalog.

You may phone in your order from
8:30–4:30 Eastern time at our toll-free number
1-800-326-7149.

Return this form to:
Princeton Book Company, Publishers
PO Box 57, Pennington, New Jersey 08534